a HAUNTING SUN

a Haunting Sun

BRENDA SCHMIDT

THISTLEDOWN PRESS

Canadian Cataloguing in Publication Data

Schmidt, Brenda, 1965 –
A haunting sun

(New leaf editions. Series seven)
ISBN 1-894345-34-7
1. Flin Flon (Man.)—Poetry. I. Title. II. Series.
PS8587.C45H38 2001   C811'.6   C2001-911003-0
PR9199.4.S35H38 2001

Book and cover design by J. Forrie
Typeset by Thistledown Press Ltd.
Printed and bound in Canada

Thistledown Press Ltd.
633 Main Street
Saskatoon, Saskatchewan
S7H 0J8

Thistledown Press gratefully acknowledges the financial assistance of the Canada Council for the Arts, the Saskatchewan Arts Board, and the Government of Canada through the Book Publishing Industry Development Program for its publishing program.

ACKNOWLEDGEMENTS

Earlier versions of some of these poems appeared in *Spring* and *Grain*.

Thanks to the Saskatchewan Writers Guild.

Thanks to Byrna Barclay, Barbara Klar, Sylvia Legris and Seán Virgo for writing comments on some of these poems during their development; Jesse Stothers, my editor, for all his work; Gerry Hill for his guidance; Judy de Mos for encouraging me daily. Thanks also to my family for their support.

Most of all, I wish to thank Harvey for his love, dedication, and for believing in me.

CONTENTS

For Harvey

Then the great Flin Flon arose, calm, dignified and grave.
— J. E. Preston Muddock, *The Sunless City*

PORTRAIT OF FLIN FLON[1]

In a word his character becomes
the flesh of this place,
features pose for the painting
wanting the strokes
of oil to smooth his expression.

Paint, he hopes, will cover
the story written in lines
between his brows,
hide the love buried in his eyes.

The image smells
of turpentine, linseed oil, dammar;
no one wants to kiss him now,
long dead, skin hanging over bones
so hard the greenstone
would break if he fell.

Paint dries a thin smile,
cracks between his lips.

[1]Flin Flon, after whom a mining town in Manitoba was named, is a fictional character in
the 1905 novel *The Sunless City*, by J. E. Preston Muddock.

CAPTURING A LANDSCAPE

The land is mined and wants
to be captured
in transparent colours,
to be tamed
with gentle brush strokes

but I trip
over a steel-toed boot.

Paint smears on rock,
covers a vein of quartz,
the flecks of gold.

INTO SUNLIT CLOUDS

Paint goes where I wish
I could go, into sunlit clouds
casting passing shadows
across the cloth of history
a pilgrimage finds
silk-soft and yellowed
under swollen knees,
so well-weaved its retelling
is jibberish in your ear.

You buy the piece because
it reminds you of home,
its colours go with yours.

Even when painted,
clouds cross the sky
in wind before a rain,
drip and drizzle
secrets on the surface
until lakes gather on the ground
to reflect until it all soaks in.

BACK CHANNEL, ATHAPAP

Don't ask when I was there,
on land I cannot speak
riddles of water and lakes
full of trophy trout.

See instead the shore I painted,
the light I caught
with my brush even
though it fought with me,

beating the breath away
from my chest, from trees
I used to trap a haunting
sun, light sinking in reeds
where perch find mouths of pike.

A solution is in the water:
ripples follow a splash
and bubbles the descent.
I am there now, in the place
the fish once was, light
hooking dead things on the bottom.

PAINTING MISTIK CREEK

All that mist obscures
the centre of interest.
The point is lost
in ripples so flat they fail
to move downstream.

Negative space disappears
in the grey blur of spruce,
branches blend rock into water.

Land, water, mind
scapes are guided
inside by a hand brushing
the ethereal. Light
dabs rouse the dark,
balance deadens the flow
against which fish run.

THIS PLACE IS JUST A PICTURE

Thousands of people
live in the six colours I squeezed
out of metal tubes, their stories
watered down, absorbed
by soft red sable.

I painted their mouths shut.

With broad strokes they became
black spruce, tamarack, bedrock
billions of years old.
Those who hate me are set free
in murky rivers, those who love
I trap in stagnant swamps.
Those I yearn to be
become sky, changing
after every wash.

It dried this way.

SETTING FIRE

Sun cuts between
the forest and the walls,
setting fire to the colour
day embraced.

Night came and held me.

Remains still smoulder
under a pile of ash.
A stick lies broken nearby.

In the dark my mouth is closed
by a hand. I learn
how to hide in painted trees.

COMPLETING THE PORTRAIT

Find the crack in the rock
where I place your face.
A finger of light points
at your nose, a sharp rock,
the nostrils two more
cracks feeding the deformed
black spruce gnawed
in the jaws of the wind.
A few stumps and sticks
scattered
all point to you.

PAINTING THE NIGHT

No one knows how to paint the night,
to capture the dead
eyes seeing rings on fingers,
knowing how to slide them
over old broken knuckles,

to part the lips so slightly
a tongue of light touches
the moist stirring
of meaning in a cast iron pot
hung low over a quiet fire,

to rest the hands on
the knees where you sit,
waiting to feel the beat
of a heart long still.

Quick fingers spread
thin cooling flesh-
tones that sing on
the shadow side.

A RENDERING

From the centre of your chest
I dig out a still dark heart.
It is a sunless city,
empty streets left
by people seeking light.
The iron gates are open,
footsteps echo
off stone buildings
moving skyward
where eyes look down
as clouds swelling
like a finger closed in a door,
darkened to a blood-pooling blue.

On the canvas it is
a grape, soon to be a raisin.
Paint imagines
the hole filling
rain falling
streets flooding
fruit folding
finally getting over itself.

AN EXTRACTION

Wind draws smooth lines
in the sand, piles
leaves and feathers against rocks.

You dig a shallow grave
for a water beetle,
make the sign of the cross.

Behind pine stands
a large smooth stone
balanced on a small one

until you raise the dead
insect from the earth, splitting
its back against the rock.

Asymmetrical blue bowl
shaped by two small hands
into a wind-warped sky
smoothed by water
warming in rotation. A circle
too predictable
might corral the clouds,
leave trees no forest and birds
no place to escape, but wild edges
reach in wetness for a space
unexplored, land
when the clay thins,
outer limits still in the air
as a wave of reasoning
finally finds shore.
There seasons melt
in the reflection, become absorbed.

OLD QUILT

Crooked stitches mar the traditional pattern,
blocks of colour fight
like she did before she died

in the dark bedroom, legs spread
exchanging her breath for a son
who was laid to rest
for screaming, for his brown eyes.

      Gin evens things out.

Sharp triangles cut
from their castaway clothes
refuse to fit together.
They scream with every stitch.

TILT

How paint runs rapt in warm white
fur of a thousand long-eared thoughts.

Held at an angle, the essence escapes,
drips off the edge, falls on hot rocks.

Crying clouds form in empty space,
wander across a paper sun. Saturated

skies do not respond to the touch
of soft hair, end the absence of colour.

Yellow and red flow into the blue,
become earth with a tilt, mud with the reversal.

A PRELIMINARY SKETCH

The guts to paint lie at my feet,
a steaming pale glistening heap,
loose, but still embodied.

Feel the way

       everything flows.

A line drawing defines
the body on the floor,
comes to life
with the addition of white.

WALKING WITH MORNING

Gravel cuts into the arch
that tries to land on light,
the sole feels the darkness.

A long walk flat-footed. Bare
white sky shivers, turning
an early breathless baby blue.

Language becomes sounds,
sharp stones slicing flesh,
letting it fall wet.

Names seep in, leaving
trees a new green
my tongue won't touch.

KILLING TIME

Rhubarb buds,
lilac blooms brown,
spring latches the gate
as summer thrusts a rusty edge
deep into everything green.

Scotch time now
before eyes blur
red from its warm amber burn.

Just a second.
A blade of grass bends
in the wind, will not rub
rough wood smooth,
fails to spread
sight thin as one
breath flattened by wind.
It only stands,

another moment wasted.
Tears wash the body,
the sun wraps it in light.

Seeds pushed into the ground
either fail to sprout or grow,
bursting from the shell
like a new idea.
They find sky as your back
turns, taking the shade
you cast, a humid shape
of darkness that shields
their silent beginning.
Moving on without seeing
life behind you,
you miss the sun
touching the newborn green
latched on the breast of night
under the blanket of morning.

WORMS

Think of worms,
guts without bodies,
moving courage without
a chest on which to pin medals
or a loved one
underneath.
Ground strokes
its soft legless spaces,
voyeurs watching
the dirty little tryst.

IN A SENSE

Lilacs scent the nose too
close to a purple so light
the petals must be final breaths
of sky and fire laid to rest.
Bees pay their respects
in the middle of stillness,
imagine honey.

I catch you kissing the back
of your hand after you eat.

Sweet green ideas
fall in the wind, blown
clear of becoming
something to want.

NEARING A DESCENT

On the edge of town a child
climbs the rocks and looks down
on old homes. Flashing eyes

beacon a loneliness that lists
too far from shore,
hole in the hull, water fills

places not seen before,
floods the dark hold.
On the way down eyes carry

weight steadily balanced,
knowing the secret
lies in well-timed blinks.

The rattle of aerosol cans, beer bottles
smashed on the ground
below. They get so high
on the rock-face, hearts
adding Dave + Leanne
for the sum of a heartache
as bright and lasting as the yellow paint.
They spray names that drip
into toeholds till they dry,
brighten the monochrome stone
they climb, the fear of falling
all but lost in the nozzle mist.

CRACKING EGGS

Birds cease to sing while they wait
to feel a crack, a separation.
They know how to walk on eggshells.

Deep in willow the sparrow nest is
dark and private, pale
blue eggs round the rounded
grass bed, feather-edged light
tastes summer, mellow
wanderings bring everything
closer to the mouth.

The first to hatch has a worm
shoved down its throat
before a sound can rise.

PUSSY WILLOW

Silk sky casts
on willow leaves
imprints of longing,
a blue-green fluttering
in the shaded flesh
of the swallowed word.

Silence sizzles,
burns through layers
of love, animosity,
between raised veins.

Wind curves the branch
like a lover's whisper,
light rocks back and forth,
tasting whatever day brings.

BLENDING IN

Red foxes are rare here, true
red phases occur in unnamed places
elsewhere.

Straight ahead, a black fox at dusk
cuts through the streetlight
into the night, comes to rest
on the edge of a swamp.
Waiting kits succour her gaunt
body lying on cold stone.

The panting tongue wets
a brush of light,
paints the town
the colour of her fur.

GARAGE SALE FINDS

A good deal, a misplaced treasure, a used object of desire.
Everything is touched, held up to the light.

A handheld mirror rimmed with gold fails to reflect
where the backing has chipped away.

A china cup used to read tea leaves cracked
from top to bottom after the child was born.

No one gives more than a dollar for anything,
less for thoughts they handle as they drink
each others stories down with cooling tea.

A NIGHT SCENE

I came here in the night
to paint tired men
walking to work
over the past, steps
crunching darkness.
Translucent intestines pour
out the stack
from an earth disembowelled,
peritoneum black,
shining. The town
a lung spotted within
a moving story, pleural
space inflamed
rubs till sparks set a blaze.
Without the guts to breathe
the idea deflates, collapses
on the canvas,
smearing the paint.

SPRING THAW

Every spring water pours from open hydrants
as they flush lines, finally runs clear

like you did when the snow stopped
falling on warm ground. The first migrant

junco foraged in your shrinking
footprints, a feathered image of love

returned, framed in a beak cracking seed.
All meaning melted

into little rivers flowing across ground
still frozen under the weak spring sun.

Ice yields to the edge of a spade,
trenches deepen with the flow.

SOME COLOURS BLEED

All pleasure seeps
slow as first blood
welling from a deep
cut. I warm with the flow,
licking all colour
from the blanching limb.

Our love tastes of salt,
pulls fluid from other spaces.

A painting waits
on the tip of my tongue,
precious red thins, starved
lips guide the strokes.

We used to love being alone,
but now I am tendrilous,
trying to climb the sky
twined around raindrops.

Each cloud is your face
changing shape, a shifting grey
idea amongst the many
blues mingling overhead.

The lightest cloud is the one
I wrap myself around.
The weight of my growing
weariness holds us together.

A TIDE OVER

I came here to find you
imprinted on white sheets,
cotton combed by tides of legs
pulled back and forth between
songs. Music calms you,

a sea wanting wind
to lift sound from a belly
so full it is green.

Sand dollars break beneath the back
of memory, fragile shards beach
as if they know our love
needs the quick snap, a blink
being too slow to miss.

STILL THE AIR

The window must be closed
before you sleep, the roaring
mine preys on the living
being proofed.

Art fills empty spaces,
painting shapes you
into smooth round buns
to rise in the night.

Hungry scratches on the glass
do not reach under sheets.
Your eyes close to the smell.

You know words the way I know
the smell of rain on wool
when I run outside to greet you

without shoes. Bare feet ache,
reminded of the rhythm
guiding the stride, the sound

of pebbles meeting underneath
your sole, the slippery click
of explanation. Gentle words

fall in my thoughts. A fullness
empties now, the last drop
lands first on my lip,

drips off bit skin and falls
in mud. Drenched, I hold
my breath, in my hand

your heavy heart beats
thunder in my bones,
a low rumble after a storm.

A LOVE SONG

If I were to kill a bird
it would be the chipping sparrow
who rings and rings but goes
unanswered, a lover
trying to say sorry
for the bit of green sky
breaking the breadth of blue.

A quick snap of the neck
between finger and thumb.

Pull off the crown
of rusty feathers,
unfold the wings,
suck the marrow from the joint
then spit it on the bald spot
where love once grew.

AT FIRST LIGHT

See how the dawn sticks
to the glass where
the chipping sparrow hit.

It flew at the window
a tiny fist knocking
on a love boarded shut,
keyhole as rusty as its crown.

Wishes failed
to break its neck.

Finally it sat swaying
on a poplar limb,
like a lingering thought
it fluttered to the ground
to scratch seeds around
dead wormy birds.

COME TO LIGHT

The sun lights a crucifix
twisted in a storm,
buries the earth beneath a shadow,

sets fire to quartz veins in greenstone,
rock curving inward
just to touch itself,

warms yellow leaves stuffed in cracks
and the backs of passing ants who move
leaf to rock to the edge of something new.

A BEAR

Police searched the night
in our yard, flashlights
hitting trees like hammers.

They concluded
the man throwing rocks
at our house was a bear.

In the morning you pick stones
off the step by the front door,
throwing them back.

A SIGN

While we have tea
the stop sign shakes
in the northwest wind,
as if afraid no one will
mind its word.

You drive an alibi
over questions,
the explanation becomes
octagonal, a dull red
tongue forming sounds
edged with white

sensibility painted over

unprimed aluminum. Two
screws secure it to a stake
longer than I need
to dig out your heart,
the whole thing capitalized.

I wish you'd quit shaking.

BINDING WOUNDS

I find time
wrapped tightly in gauze,
the distal end swollen blue.

There are ways to dress wounds,
but this is not one.

You rub your finger
against the hangnail on your thumb,
passing wool without needles,
without wool. Those hands knit
hours into years

but refuse to unwind the bandage
when the bleeding stops,
allow the pulse to fade.

IN THE WIND

The ground swells
belly shifting
like a thrush's song.

Rake the memories in a pile
to bag before they scatter
in the first spring breeze.

See how the mind blows
dry sand into dunes
in the middle of the prairie.

When the wind dies
a vesper sparrow picks
heavy seeds left behind.

ORGANIC MATTER

Compost exhales after turning,
sweet and rotting breath
thick as rope and stronger.

Crawl under coffee grounds,
eggshells, carrot peels.
Dig through the chopped grass

and shredded leaves. Lie down
beside me, your body will
flesh my buried bone.

BEYOND EXPECTATION

In the hours we wait heat swells
like flesh around a bubble
of blood drawn by a sandfly.

We sit on opposite ends
of the couch in the sunroom
joined by the fingers

of a breeze. A raven croaks,
lands in our garden, watches
you cross fingers I know

as well as the Lord's Prayer.
Sun separates poplar leaves
to point at the nick in the screen

where the cat and mosquito met
last Sunday. Now fungus gnats
move through, rosary beads with wings.

NIGHT WEARS MY CAT

During the day
it lies on the track
of sun, purrs
when run over
by the bright steel
light, loves the derailing.

Lazy paws wipe
off the white meat
of moonlight stuck,
crusted, in the corner
of its fur-lined mouth.

The cat eyes my breath,
sucking all the warmth
from my chest to soothe
its bone-scratched throat.

RECALL

Dreams say little more than leaves
in a teacup left from last evening.

The chipping sparrow trills
like it did yesterday,
a telephone with no one
waiting on the other end.

I want to pick it up and speak,
sipping on the morning light,
but it runs out the side of my mouth
when I answer.

SWEET BASIL

Flavour my final days,
smell touch me
still as night breathes.

Hungry, cling
like those green aphids
piled on the underside of leaves
left shrivelling in the sun.

WORDS ARE RAVENS

All day your words are ravens
riding sunlit thermals
skimming rock faces
bored deep by men
seeking more ore.

All night ravens rest in trees
listen to the rumble underground
to owls calling from black spruce
or to soft mice dying
in beaks shredding fur and flesh,
knowing talons won't let go.

ROAD KILL

In the morning ditches draw ravens,

black bills dipping deep
in the belly of a doe

as if they knew
the fetus would be tender.

Between swallows low croaks
fill the emptied space.

SLAG DUMP

Sit on the face
of basalt rock,
cold licks between
us, two pairs of lips

touch in the curling
air, as the night
pushes and expels
the past all around.

Watch souls rise,
metal from ore,
as molten slag hits
cool tailings.

Feel the earth shake
when the train returns
for more remains. Listen
as rock falls underground.

AN OPENING

in dark colours
worn loose
flowing over the body
of a thought,

fingers slip into warm folds,
nub rubbed raw
yens for the tongue,
the thrum of the silk shod moon.

EVERY TIME IT RAINS

You go out alone
to stand as drops fall
and bead on your face.

Tonight you sit drenched in mud,
looking at me
like a statue or a word
I do not know.

I lead you in, peel your skin,
wet flesh an acid
sweet orange so ripe
you drip when pulled apart.

Even in the dark
I can feel the bruises
where you were squeezed.

MIDNIGHT

You wear a green gown
the cat chews.
A hairball lands
on your breastbone
then slips down a rib.

The moon licks
bare clavicles
before going down.

Your pelvis is narrow,
dirt covered, snakes
slide by, shine bone.

Light peeks at you,
plays with itself,
night's white dripping.

NIGHT IS OBESE

Night suck the marrow of silence
from the warm bones of grouse,
swallow the wing's hollow drum,
lick the log it roosts above
its eyes filled with mooncream,
honey-glazed feathers dripping down.

GAME

Sing with the river,
quiet the howling child.
Watch death scraping
the skin off the wind
hanging flesh to dry
smoked and cured
over posts hewn green.

The animal stiffens
before it is skinned.
The hide peels off easily
compared to the one
skinned alive,
muzzle tied shut,
gut tight with swallowed howls.

The meat is tough,
our tongues a swollen unholy red.
We sit in the dark and chew.

DRAWING MY LAST BREATH

An axe cuts me loose
from the present.
Night tightens fear

around my neck,
drags me
behind a dark horse,

pins my body
like paper to a board
as monsters stir

pots of children
until there is light.
In the morning

the first breath I draw
leaves me nearly white
against the trees,

the last throws my lungs
across the sun,
shadows spot the ground.

MORNING ALWAYS FOLLOWS

A cat meowing
on the heels of a dogless man,
stopping to sniff deer tracks
but not following

the trail knowing deer
offer nothing to the hunter
who lost half an ear
in the belly of night.

AS NIGHT PASSES

The time between each laboured breath
is a sketch, a drawing, a masterpiece,
a warm chicken gizzard blue.

Lips give air
something to stroke
on its way through,
seeking moist
places to enter
and lick after
the lines are drawn.